ECO-ACTION

Energy
of the Future

Angela Royston

Heinemann
LIBRARY

www.heinemann.co.uk/library
Visit our website to find out more information about **Heinemann Library** books.

To order:
☎ Phone 44 (0) 1865 888066
🖹 Send a fax to 44 (0) 1865 314091
💻 Visit the Heinemann Bookshop at **www.heinemann.co.uk/library** to browse our catalogue and order online.

First published in Great Britain by Heinemann Library, Halley Court, Jordan Hill, Oxford OX2 8EJ, part of Harcourt Education.
Heinemann is a registered trademark of Harcourt Education Ltd.

Editorial: Catherine Veitch and Melanie Waldron
Design: Philippa Jenkins and Michelle Lisseter
Illustrations: Bridge Creative Services p.8;
    Jeff Edwards p.43; Philippa Jenkins pp.5, 6,
    12, 17; Mark Preston p.23; Gary Slater pp.10, 28;
    David West Children's Books pp.20, 24, 26, 30
Picture Research: Melissa Allison
Production: Alison Parsons

Originated by Chroma Graphics (Overseas) Pte. Ltd .
Printed and bound in China by South China Printing Co. Ltd.

ISBN 978 0 4310 2989 4
12 11 10 09
10 9 8 7 6 5 4 3 2

British Library Cataloguing in Publication Data
Royston, Angela
Energy of the future. - (Eco-action)
333.7'94

A full catalogue record for this book is available from the British Library.

Acknowledgements
The publishers would like to thank the following for permission to reproduce photographs:
©Alamy pp. **36** (G P Bowater), **19** (Mark Baigent), **9** (Mark Pearson), **35** (Phil Degginger), **40** (Simon Belcher); ©Stock Connection Distribution p. **18** (Craig Cozart); ©Ballard Power Systems p. **34**; ©Corbis pp. **11** (Louie Psihoyos), **13** (Paul Hardy); ©Corbis/Australian Picture Library p. **29** (John Carnemolla); ©Corbis/Reuters pp. **31** (Lee Jae-Won), **37** (Mario Anzuoni); ©Corbis Sygma p. **22** (Attar Maher); ©Empics/AP Photo p. **21** (Xinhua, Du Huaju); ©Getty Images/Photonica/ PicturePress p. **15**; ©Masterfile p. **4** (Zoran Milich); ©NASA p. **32**; ©OnAsia Images p. **14** (David Dare Parker); ©Science Photo Library pp. **33** (EFDA-JET), **27** (Peter Menzel); ©Still Pictures p. **7** (M. Franken); ©UPPA p. **25** (Photoshot).

Cover photograph of a solar power panel, Nevada, USA, reproduced with permission of Masterfile/Steve Craft.

Every effort has been made to contact copyright holders of any material reproduced in this book. Any omissions will be rectified in subsequent printings if notice is given to the publishers.

Disclaimer
All the internet addresses (URLs) given in this book were valid at time of going to press. However, due to the dynamic nature of the Internet, some addresses may have changed, or sites may have changed or ceased to exist since publication. While the author and publishers regret any inconvenience this may cause readers, no responsibility for any such changes can be accepted by either the author or the publishers. It is recommended that adults supervise children on the Internet.

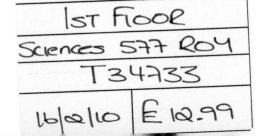

Contents

Any words appearing in the text in bold, **like this**, are explained in the Glossary.

Global challenge

People in Europe, North America, and other **developed countries** are enjoying higher standards of living. Today most families own a car and can afford to travel by air. In fact, many families own two or more cars and drive almost everywhere they go. Central heating, air conditioning, washing machines, dishwashers, and a host of other electrical goods make life easier. Personal computers, DVD players, and mobile phones are just some of the most recent inventions that make life more fun. The design, manufacture, and sales of all these consumer goods provide jobs for millions of people. As people's lives become busier, they rely on cars, air travel, and electrical machines to save them time. These things save time, but they use energy.

Consuming energy and materials

Energy is the power to do something. Cars, aeroplanes, and other vehicles burn **fuel** made from oil. All the gadgets and machines used at home, in school, and at work run on electricity that comes either from batteries or through the mains from **power stations**. Most power stations burn coal, oil, or **natural gas** to make electricity. These fuels are part of the Earth's **resources**, as are the materials that are used to make the cars, computers, cookers, clothes, and everything else we buy and use.

Most electricity comes directly to towns and cities through overhead power lines like these.

21st century challenge

People in developed countries make up only a quarter of the Earth's population but they are consuming most of the Earth's resources. It would not be possible for everyone in the world to have a similar standard of living to people in developed countries – the Earth does not have enough resources. For everyone to live as the average person in the United States does, for example, would require more than five planets just like Earth to supply the energy and materials. So far, however, most people consume much less than this. If everyone lived as the average person in India does, we could manage with just a quarter of the Earth's resources.

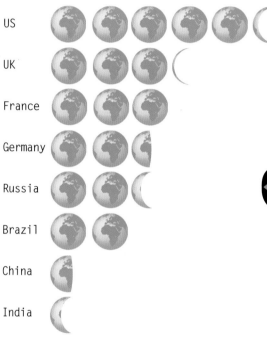

US

UK

France

Germany

Russia

Brazil

China

India

This diagram shows how many planet Earths would be needed if everyone in the world had the same standard of living as the average person in these countries.

As well as consuming far more than their fair share of the Earth's resources, the way of life in developed countries is causing a huge problem. It is called **global warming** and it is the biggest challenge facing the world. To meet this challenge, people in richer countries must change the way they generate electricity in the future and the way they live now. If they don't, the world will suffer increasing catastrophes throughout the 21st century.

BURNING ELECTRICITY
Electricity is measured in watts, kilowatts, and **megawatts**. Most electric light bulbs are 100 watts. The average U.S. home burns about 10,000 kilowatt-hours per year. Each megawatt generated by a power station supplies electricity for up to 300 U.S. homes.

Global warming

Global warming is a rise in the average temperature worldwide. Some places are always hotter than others, but over the last 100 years the average temperature at the surface of the Earth has increased by 0.8 °Celsius (1.4 °Fahrenheit). Although this increase sounds small it is changing climates around the world and causing more extreme weather.

This graph shows how the average temperature of the Earth rose between 1900 and 2006.

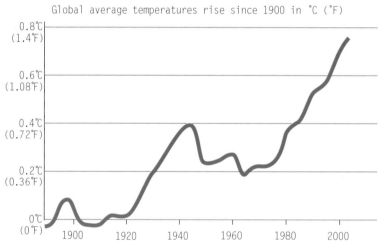

Global average temperatures rise since 1900 in °C (°F)

Climate change

Summer heatwaves have become more common in both the northern and southern hemispheres. The ten hottest years have all occurred in the last 15 years and, in some countries, the average temperature for 2006 was the hottest on record. Storms, such as hurricanes and typhoons, have become more common and more severe. Most of the rise in world temperature has occurred during the last 30 years and scientists say that if the temperature continues to rise at the present rate it will cause increasing catastrophes, including famines, disease, the wiping out of many species, and coastal flooding.

What could happen as the temperature of the Earth warms	
by 1°C (1.8°F)	• Warmer seas mean that 80% of coral reefs begin to die. • 10% of species could become extinct due to changes in habitats. • Water becomes increasingly scarce, threatening the lives of 50 million people.
by 2°C (3.6°F) *This could happen by 2050 or sooner.*	• Water from melting glaciers pours into the oceans, causing the sea level to rise by up to 20 cm (8 inches). • Polar bears and caribou become extinct. • In Africa 60 million more people could catch malaria.
by 3°C (5.4°F)	• Up to 40% of species threatened with extinction. • Up to 4 billion people could suffer from water shortages. • Southern Europe becomes semi-desert. • More than 100 million people who live on the coast threatened by floods.
by 4°C (7.2°F)	• Australia becomes too hot for wheat and other farm crops to grow. • Antarctic ice sheets begin to melt, causing further rise in sea level. • Agricultural output in Africa decreases by 15–35%.
by 5°C (9°F) *This could happen by 2100.*	• About half of the world's biggest cities, including London, New York, and Tokyo, are seriously flooded as sea level rises by up to 12 m (40 ft). • Billions of people move inland from the coast and to other countries. • Hundreds of millions of people in China and India are short of water.

South-eastern Spain already suffers from serious droughts. If global warming continues unchecked, much of the Mediterranean and lands south of the Sahara could become semi-desert.

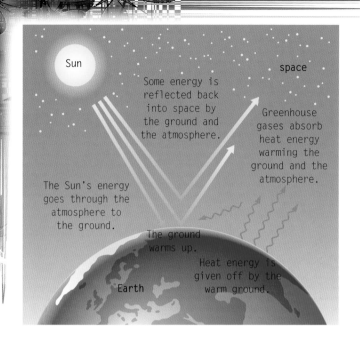

Sun

space

Some energy is reflected back into space by the ground and the atmosphere.

Greenhouse gases absorb heat energy warming the ground and the atmosphere.

The Sun's energy goes through the atmosphere to the ground.

The ground warms up.

Heat energy is given off by the warm ground.

Earth

Gases in the air absorb heat that would otherwise escape into space. They make the surface of the Earth warmer.

What causes global warming?

Gases in the air trap the Sun's heat and cause global warming. The gases act like a greenhouse – they make the air near the Earth's surface hotter than it would otherwise be. They are known as **greenhouse gases**.

The Sun's energy

Energy in the form of light and heat from the Sun falls on to the Earth's surface. Much of the heat is absorbed by the land and sea and the rest is reflected back into the air. The heat that has been absorbed also escapes through the air and back into space. This keeps a balance between the heat received and the heat lost. Greenhouse gases, however, trap a small amount of heat, slowly raising the temperature of the Earth by a small amount. **Carbon dioxide** is the most common of the damaging greenhouse gases.

Greenhouse gases

The main greenhouse gases are carbon dioxide, **water vapour**, **methane**, and **nitrous oxide**. Water vapour is essential as it is part of the **water cycle**, which we rely on for rain. Carbon dioxide is produced naturally but humans are now adding billions of extra tonnes of carbon dioxide to the air. Excess methane and nitrous oxide are mostly produced by modern farming methods.

Carbon cycle

All living things breathe out carbon dioxide. They also produce carbon dioxide when they die and decompose or are burned. Trees and all green plants take in carbon dioxide from the air. They use the energy of sunlight to combine carbon dioxide from the air with water from the soil to make food. This process is called **photosynthesis**. Living things, therefore, emit and take in carbon dioxide, so the amount of carbon dioxide in the air should stay about the same. The problem comes from extra carbon dioxide produced by burning coal, oil, and natural gas.

Coal, oil, and natural gas

In the last 100 years humans have been burning more and more coal, oil, and natural gas. Motor cars and aeroplanes – which burn fuel made from oil – were invented just over 100 years ago and, in the last 40 to 50 years, have become increasingly affordable and widely used. In the last 60 years or so, the mass production of electrical goods has improved the standard of living in developed countries, pushing up the demand for electricity. This means that more coal, oil, and natural gas are being burned in power stations.

Real greenhouses can be useful. In cooler countries many tropical plants can only grow in the hotter atmosphere of a greenhouse.

9

Fossil fuels

Coal, oil, and natural gas are called **fossil fuels** because they were formed millions of years ago. They were formed from the remains of forests and millions of tiny sea creatures that lived 300 million years ago, even longer ago than the dinosaurs. When the forests and sea creatures died they were covered by layer after layer of **silt**. As the silt built up, the buried plants were crushed and gradually became coal and natural gas. Similarly the sea animals became oil and natural gas.

Mining coal and oil

Coal and oil are often found deep under the ground and under the seabed. Much of the coal is cut from mines near the surface, but elsewhere deep shafts are dug through the rock so that miners can cut out the coal and bring it to the surface. Today, coal is mostly used to generate electricity.

Oil is piped or transported from an oil well to a **refinery** where it is heated to separate it into many different substances, including petrol, kerosene (aircraft fuel), and diesel oil. Oil provides fuel for transport, central heating, and for oil-burning power stations. It is also used to make **synthetic materials** of all kinds, including plastics, nylon, acrylic materials, and polystyrene.

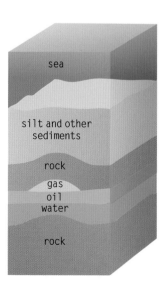

When the remains of tiny sea creatures are crushed and trapped between layers of rock, they slowly change into oil and natural gas.

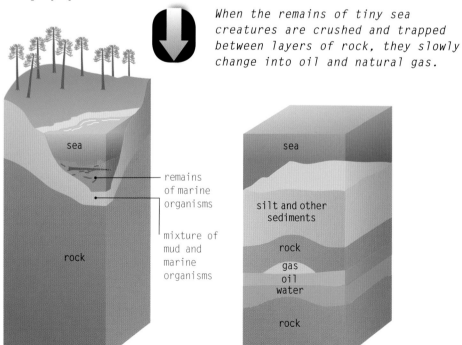

sea

remains of marine organisms

mixture of mud and marine organisms

rock

sea

silt and other sediments

rock

gas

oil

water

rock

Natural gas

Natural gas is methane. It formed at the same time as coal and oil and is trapped between layers of rock. At first natural gas was burned off at the oil well as a waste gas. Now people realize that it is a better fuel than oil because it produces less carbon dioxide and other pollutants. Natural gas is piped to power stations to generate electricity, and to buildings where it is used mainly for central heating and cooking.

Carbon stores

Like living things, coal, oil, and natural gas are composed mainly of carbon and hydrogen. When living things die, the carbon in their bodies is released as carbon dioxide but, when fossil fuels formed, the carbon was trapped underground and stored instead. Carbon burns well and so makes a good fuel, but as it burns it combines with oxygen from the air to make carbon dioxide.

A NEW SOURCE OF FUEL?

Huge deposits of **gas hydrates** – slushy mixtures of ice with methane trapped in them – have been found under the seabed. Could they provide a vast new source of natural gas? Some scientists think so, but others are concerned that mining them would allow large amounts of methane to escape into the air. This would speed up global warming because, as a greenhouse gas, methane is 20 times more powerful than carbon dioxide.

Coal is loaded on to coal wagons and taken by rail to power stations.

How generating electricity contributes to global warming

Fossil fuels are burned to produce energy. Oil powers almost all vehicles and natural gas heats homes and cookers. Coal, oil, and natural gas are all used in power stations to generate electricity. This produces more carbon dioxide than any other activity and, since 1990, the emissions from power stations have been growing faster than from any other source.

Who needs electricity?

In developed countries, everyone uses electricity. It is used in homes for lighting and to run every electrical machine from refrigerators, freezers, washing machines, and dishwashers to computers, CD players, and hair dryers. Schools, hospitals, offices, and other large buildings use electricity for lighting and air conditioning and to run equipment, such as computers, photocopiers, fax machines, and medical equipment in hospitals. In shops, electricity powers lighting, cool cabinets, and freezers, while machinery in factories consumes large amounts of electricity to make goods of all kinds.

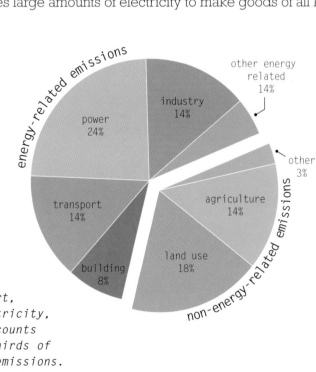

Energy (transport, generating electricity, and heating) accounts for about two-thirds of carbon dioxide emissions. The remaining third comes from agriculture, the destruction of forests, and waste disposal.

*Electricity is fed from this power station into a **grid** of electricity cables.*

How a power station works

Most power stations burn fossil fuels. They use the fuel to heat water to make steam that drives a **turbine** to generate electricity. It takes huge amounts of fuel to generate enough electricity to supply each country, and that, of course, creates huge amounts of carbon dioxide. Although different companies may supply electricity, the distribution is organized across each state or country. Cables carry the electricity to every building, traffic light, street light, and wherever electricity is used.

Increasing demand

Demand for electricity has grown not only in developed countries but in other countries too. China, a country with a population of more than 1,000 million people, is **industrializing** fast. Many of the electronic goods, clothes, toys, and other items you buy are now manufactured in China in thousands of factories that consume ever more electricity. To supply the extra demand, about 50 new power stations are being built every year, which is equivalent to one a week. China has large deposits of coal, so these power stations mostly burn coal, the most polluting fossil fuel. China is not the only country that is developing fast. India, whose population is also about 1,000 million people, and countries such as Indonesia in South-East Asia are also industrializing.

Electricity for the future

The amount of fossil fuel burnt needs to be substantially reduced. It needs to be reduced in all areas of energy, but this book looks specifically at how electricity can be generated while producing much less or no carbon dioxide. The good news is that the technology to do this is already being developed.

Carbon-free energy

The following chapters show how water, wind, and the Sun can all be used to generate electricity. Once they are built and running, these generators produce no carbon dioxide or other greenhouse gas. They are called "**renewable**" sources of energy because the source of their energy will never run out. Some people claim that nuclear power is a **carbon-free** source of energy, but nuclear power involves huge problems (see pages 30–31) and it is neither renewable nor carbon-free.

Cleaner energy from fossil fuels

Some people argue that renewable sources of energy can never supply all the electricity that is needed and that we will still need power stations that burn fossil fuels. If so, the emissions from fossil fuels need to be reduced. One way to do this is to replace coal and oil-fired power stations with ones that burn natural gas. Natural gas produces twice as much energy for the same amount of carbon dioxide as coal.

A gas pipeline being laid in Western Australia in 1997. Natural gas is the most efficient fossil fuel and causes the least pollution.

This is a combined heat and power plant. It uses "waste" steam to heat buildings in the surrounding area.

Reducing waste

In a traditional coal-fired power station only about a quarter of the energy available in fossil fuels actually reaches your home as electricity. More than 60 percent of it is lost as heat in the power station and the rest in transmission through the grid – a complex network of electricity cables. A new kind of local power station called a **CHP** (combined heat and power) plant uses the waste heat from generating electricity to heat buildings in the local area. Most CHP plants burn natural gas or coal.

Another way to reduce waste is to rely less on the grid and produce more electricity locally. CHP plants are well suited for this, as are renewables. Denmark already generates half of its electricity locally, while CHP provides over 90 percent of the heating for Helsinki, the capital city of Finland.

FUTURISTIC OR FANTASTICAL?
Instead of tackling global warming by reducing carbon dioxide emissions, one inventor suggests huge mirrors should be put in space to reflect the Sun's rays before they reach Earth. The mirrors, however, would need to be vast and would be unbelievably expensive. It would be much better to spend the money on renewable sources of energy.

15

Wind power

Wind can be a powerful **force** and is a renewable source of energy. In the past windmills used wind power to grind corn and they are still used in places to pump water. Today a new kind of windmill, called a **wind turbine**, offers a never-ending source of carbon-free energy.

Wind turbines

Most wind turbines have three thin blades that rotate like the blades of a helicopter. The blades can be very long – up to nearly 90 metres (295 feet) at present – and are attached to a **hub**, mounted on the top of a tall, hollow tower, or pylon. The spinning blades turn a shaft inside the hub and a generator uses this movement to make electricity. The hub swivels so that the blades are always at the best angle to the wind. A computer inside the hub monitors the speed and direction of the wind and controls the direction and angle of the blades. If the wind becomes too strong, it will even slow the blades down so that they are not damaged. Electrical cables carry away the electricity.

Size of turbines

The size of a wind turbine varies from small ones that go on top of a house to the largest ones, which can be erected out at sea. A small turbine can only generate enough electricity to power a few lights, but the largest can generate 4–5 megawatts (4–5 million watts) each.

WHAT DRIVES THE WIND?

The Sun heats some parts of the Earth's surface more than others and these differences create wind. Warm air rises, and as it does so it pulls in cooler air from round about – the moving air is wind. Places in the tropics get the most heat, while places close to the poles get the least. Land warms up faster than the sea, and valleys are usually warmer than hilltops.

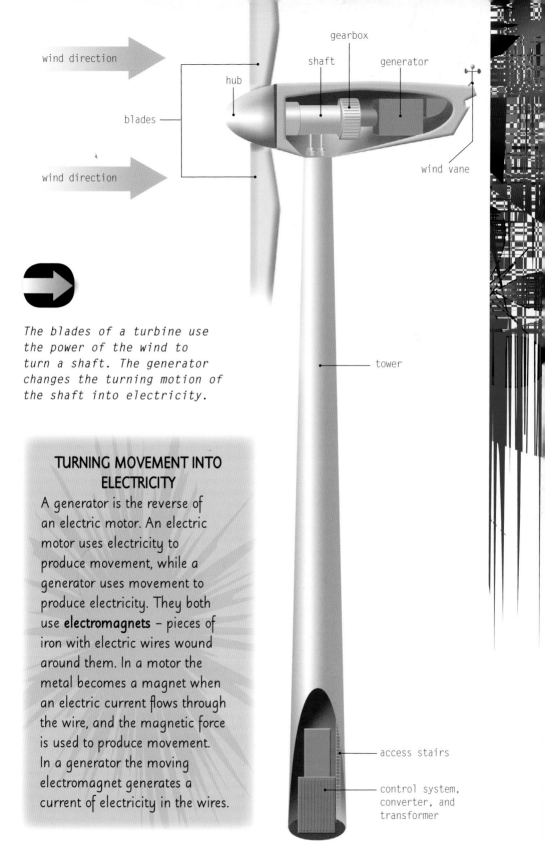

wind direction

hub

blades

wind direction

gearbox

shaft

generator

wind vane

tower

➡

The blades of a turbine use the power of the wind to turn a shaft. The generator changes the turning motion of the shaft into electricity.

TURNING MOVEMENT INTO ELECTRICITY

A generator is the reverse of an electric motor. An electric motor uses electricity to produce movement, while a generator uses movement to produce electricity. They both use **electromagnets** – pieces of iron with electric wires wound around them. In a motor the metal becomes a magnet when an electric current flows through the wire, and the magnetic force is used to produce movement. In a generator the moving electromagnet generates a current of electricity in the wires.

access stairs

control system, converter, and transformer

17

This wind farm is in Altamont Pass, California, U.S.A. Some people complain that wind farms are noisy so wind turbines should not be erected close to homes.

Wind farms

A wind farm is a group of several wind turbines. Some wind farms have fewer than 10 turbines, but the largest have several hundred. Wind turbines only work when the wind is blowing of course, so they should be placed where there is a strong, steady wind at all times of the year.

Best sites for wind farms

The tops of hills and the coast are often windy, but another good place for wind turbines is offshore, where the wind is stronger and bigger turbines can be built. A wind farm occupies a lot of space because the turbines cannot be placed too close to each other in case they shelter each other from the wind. The coasts of Britain are particularly suitable for wind farms and in the future they could become a common sight here. The prairies in the United States and Canada are windy too. The U.S. states of Texas, Minnesota, and Iowa already have several large wind farms. In Europe, wind farms are well established in many countries, from Portugal to Germany and Denmark.

CAPE WIND

The company Cape Wind is planning to build a wind farm on Nantucket Sound in Massachusetts, U.S.A. It will have 130 turbines and supply up to 450 megawatts of electricity. On an averagely windy day, the turbines will supply Cape Cod and the Islands with three-quarters of the electricity they need. The construction of the turbines is planned to begin in 2010.

Scroby Sands is a wind farm with 30 turbines, just off the coast of Yarmouth in eastern England. Tourists are drawn to the town to admire their graceful shapes. The turbines save 75,000 tonnes of carbon dioxide being released into the atmosphere each year from a conventional power station.

ALIEN OR ARTISTIC?

Wind farms are often built on islands and other remote places. Some local people protest that the huge turbines ruin their landscape. They say that the turbines look alien. Other people like the elegant shape of wind turbines and see them as a form of modern sculpture. Do you think people should have to accept wind farms in their areas?

Water power

Flowing water is a powerful force – you just need to hold your hand under a tap to feel it. Imagine the power of a huge mass of fast-moving water! Flowing water is a renewable source of energy that produces no carbon dioxide or other greenhouse gases when it is used to generate electricity. There are three different ways of using water to generate electricity – hydroelectric, tidal, and wave power. The most established of these is hydroelectric power.

Hydroelectric power

When a massive amount of water tries to squeeze through a narrow gap, it produces a very large force. This is the force that a hydroelectric power station harnesses. A dam is built across a river to form a lake. The dam has to be made of thick concrete to be strong enough to hold back the lake of water. A stream of water is fed through a tunnel, which goes from the bottom of the lake, under the dam to the power station where the turbines are. The force of the flowing water spins the turbines and so generates electricity.

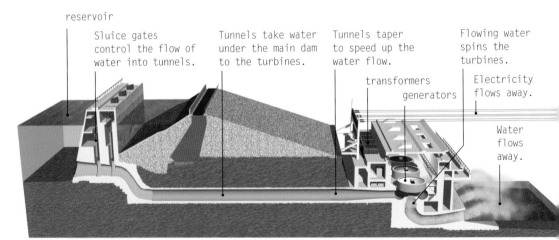

reservoir

Sluice gates control the flow of water into tunnels.

Tunnels take water under the main dam to the turbines.

Tunnels taper to speed up the water flow.

Flowing water spins the turbines.

transformers

generators

Electricity flows away.

Water flows away.

This is how a hydroelectric power station works. It is very efficient, converting about 90 percent of the water's energy into electricity.

Good sites for hydroelectricity

A mountain gorge is a good place for a hydroelectric power station because only a short dam needs to be built across it to form a deep reservoir. Both New Zealand and Norway use hydroelectric power stations to generate most of their electricity. The largest hydroelectric power station, Three Gorges Dam in China, has been built across the River Yangtze, and by 2009 it is hoped that it will generate more than 10 percent of China's electricity. Most countries with mountains have some hydroelectric power stations.

Advantages and disadvantages

Once a hydroelectric power station is built, it produces no carbon dioxide. The lake stores so much water it never runs dry even during droughts, giving a reliable supply of electricity. The lake is often used as a reservoir, supplying piped water to millions of people. One huge advantage of the Three Gorges Dam is that it stops the River Yangtze flooding further downstream – such floods killed more than a million people last century.

The main disadvantage of hydroelectric power is that a whole valley is flooded to make the lake, and the people who live there have to leave their homes. Stopping the river flooding is not always an advantage. The River Nile, for example, used to flood at certain times of the year, irrigating farmland on each bank. This no longer happens, making it harder to grow crops. Although the power station is carbon-free once it is running, building the thick concrete dam is expensive and creates tonnes of carbon dioxide.

The Three Gorges Dam in China holds back a lake around 645 kilometres (400 miles) long that powers a huge hydroelectric power station.

Tidal power

The level of the sea rises and falls, giving two high tides and two low tides per day at the coast. The difference between high and low tide is usually less than 4 metres (13 feet) but in some places the difference is much greater. A **tidal power station** uses the flow of the water produced by the changing tides to generate electricity.

How a tidal power station works

The best place for a tidal power station is across a bay or river estuary where the rise and fall of the tide can give a difference of 8 metres (26 feet) or more in sea level. A barrage built across the estuary acts like a dam in a hydroelectric power station, with the water flowing through the barrage to form a large lake and then out again. As the tide comes in, the incoming water turns the turbine to generate electricity. The water is trapped behind the barrage and then released through the turbine again as the tide falls, generating more electricity.

The first tidal power station was built at La Rance in France in the 1960s and it is still the world's leading tidal power station. A smaller tidal power plant has been built in the Bay of Fundy in Canada to take advantage of its huge tidal difference of up to 16 metres (52 feet), and tidal projects have been set up in Russia and China.

La Rance near St Malo in France was revolutionary in its day, but such tidal schemes are still very expensive.

This is an artist's impression of what a tidal farm would look like. It has advantages over both land-based wind farms and tidal barrages.

TIDAL FARMS

One idea for the future is to build **tidal stream farms**. Turbines are sunk below water in places where there are fast-moving tides or currents. They generate electricity under water in much the same way as wind turbines do in the air (see pages 16–17) but they have the advantages of being mostly out of sight, having little effect on the environment, and being as totally reliable as the tides.

Advantages and disadvantages

The biggest advantage of a tidal power station is that it produces carbon-free energy, but building the concrete and earth barrage is expensive and creates tonnes of carbon dioxide. The supply of electricity varies at different times of the day, according to the state of the tide.

The barrage acts as a bridge spanning the estuary, but it evens out the flow of the tide, which means that mud flats and salt marshes that used to be exposed at low tide are under water much longer. Environmentalists usually oppose the building of a tidal barrage because they say it threatens the habitat of birds and other wildlife that inhabit the estuary.

Wave power

The movement of waves is a renewable and carbon-free source of energy. It is easy to see the power of the sea in the waves that crash on to the shore, but it is not quite so easy to harness that power into a cheap and reliable source of electricity. Waves vary in size from ripples to huge rollers 12 metres (40 feet) or more high, so wave-power generators have to be strong enough to withstand a considerable battering. Several different schemes have been tried and new ideas are being developed.

ISLAY WAVE POWER STATION

The first viable wave power generator is situated on the coast of the island of Islay in Scotland. As the waves enter the generator they push air out of a chamber. As the wave recedes, air is pulled back into the chamber. The movement of the air drives a turbine that is used to generate electricity. The device on Islay produces enough power for the nearby village, but the supply varies according to the weather and the tides.

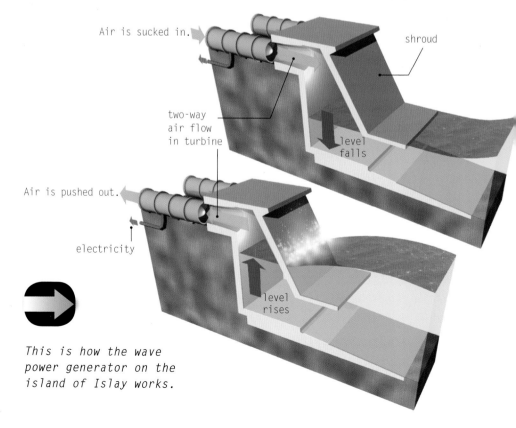

Air is sucked in.

shroud

two-way
air flow
in turbine

level
falls

Air is pushed out.

electricity

level
rises

This is how the wave power generator on the island of Islay works.

Salter's ducks

Professor Stephen Salter, a British engineer, invented one of the first wave power technologies to be developed. Curved floats, known as "ducks", tilt up and down in the waves, driving turbines that generate electricity very efficiently. Unfortunately the project was dropped in the 1980s when a European Union report estimated the cost of the electricity they produced to be 10 times greater that it actually was. Since the mistake was realized in the early 2000s, people are looking again at Salter's ducks.

The Pelamis project

The **Pelamis wave energy converter** uses the power of the ocean swell. It consists of several sections that ride the swell, floating half above and half below the water. The sections are joined by hinges and it is the movement at the hinges that is used to turn the turbines that generate electricity. The electricity is fed through an electrical cable from the nose of the structure down to the seabed and back to the shore. Several *Pelamis* converters, moored about 5–20 kilometres from the shore, can be used together in a wave farm. The first commercial use of *Pelamis* began in 2006 off the coast of Portugal.

This is an artist's impression of how the Pelamis *wave energy converter might look. The name* Pelamis *means "sea snake".*

Advantages and disadvantages

In many parts of the world wave power offers an opportunity for carbon-free energy. It is estimated that Britain, for example, could generate a quarter of all the electricity it needs from the waves. Offshore generators could be a hazard to ships, however, and many people still believe it is too expensive to make them strong enough to survive storms.

Solar power

The Sun is the largest source of renewable energy. Every day enough energy reaches the Earth to provide us with many times the amount we need in a year. The energy is spread out, however, and has to be collected and concentrated before it can be used to generate electricity. That is what a **CSP** (concentrated solar power) station does.

How CSP stations work

Solar power stations use curved mirrors to concentrate the heat of the Sun. There are different ways of doing this. In one, the mirrors focus the heat on a central collector at the top of a tall tower. The temperature of the collector can reach up to 565 °C (almost 1,050 °F). This heat is transferred via a heat exchanger to boil water and make steam, which drives a turbine. Tanks of molten salt are used to store excess heat so that the power station can go on working after the Sun has set.

In another design, the mirrors are arranged in long troughs. The Sun's heat is reflected on to a pipe containing oil that runs along the middle of the trough. The heated oil is piped to the power station where it is used to drive a steam turbine. This design is often used along with a power station that burns natural gas to generate electricity after dark.

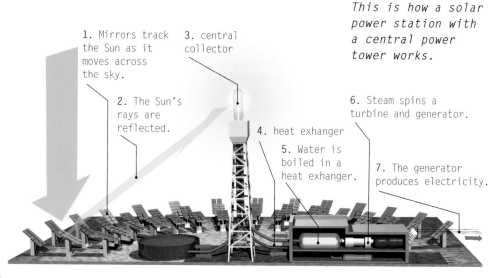

This is how a solar power station with a central power tower works.

1. Mirrors track the Sun as it moves across the sky.

2. The Sun's rays are reflected.

3. central collector

4. heat exhanger

5. Water is boiled in a heat exhanger.

6. Steam spins a turbine and generator.

7. The generator produces electricity.

This solar
power plant in Barstow,
California, U.S.A, has a central
power tower to collect the Sun's heat.

Bigger and better

The hot deserts north and south of the equator are the best places for solar power stations. The Sun is much stronger here than elsewhere and there is plenty of space for them. California in the United States has a CSP in the Mojave Desert that has been generating electricity for more than 15 years. More are being built in the U.S. state of Nevada, in Australia, and southern Spain.

Disadvantages and advantages

The main disadvantage of solar power is that there is no sunlight at night, which is why solar power stations either work in combination with natural gas power stations or have a tank to store excess heat. Waste heat can be used to **desalinate** water – particularly useful in the desert. The mirrors, which can take up a great deal of space, can also be used to advantage in the desert by providing shade for crops that are irrigated with the desalinated water.

PHOTOVOLTAIC CELLS
Photovoltaic cells use sunlight to generate electricity. They already supply electricity to many individual buildings and are used to power spacecraft in space. They will become more common in future and will even be able to supply whole towns and cities.

Nuclear power

Huge amounts of energy are locked up in the smallest units of matter – **atoms**. When an atom is split it releases some of that energy. Nuclear energy was first used in the uncontrolled explosions of two atomic bombs that destroyed the Japanese cities of Hiroshima and Nagasaki towards the end of World War II. Soon after the war the technology was adapted to release a controlled supply of heat to drive a turbine to generate electricity. Now nuclear power stations generate about 15 percent of the world's electricity, but their use is very controversial.

Anatomy of an atom

Every substance is composed of atoms, which contain three kinds of complex particles – **electrons**, **protons**, and **neutrons**. Protons and neutrons form a nucleus around which the electrons orbit, rather like the planets orbit the Sun. A nuclear force holds the particles together and it is this force that scientists unleash when they split an atom. The atom they use is **uranium** because its nucleus is less stable than other atoms and is easier to split.

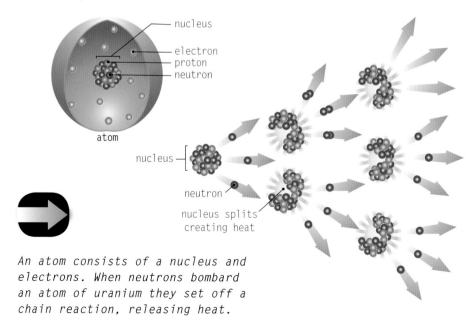

An atom consists of a nucleus and electrons. When neutrons bombard an atom of uranium they set off a chain reaction, releasing heat.

This uranium mine is in Kakadu, Australia. Uranium mines can damage the environment and the health of the people who work in them.

Uranium

Uranium is a very heavy metal that is mined from rocks. Although uranium occurs in all rocks, there is too little in most rocks to make it worth mining. The main uranium mines that supply the nuclear industry are in Canada, Australia, Kazakhstan, Russia, Namibia, and Niger. Even here the uranium is so thinly spread that huge amounts of rock have to be processed to extract a small amount of it. The process produces many tonnes of waste and carbon dioxide.

Uranium exists in different forms called **isotopes**. One isotope is particularly unstable. When one of its atoms is bombarded by neutrons, the nucleus breaks into two, creating heat and releasing spare neutrons. This process is called **nuclear fission**. These neutrons then bombard another atom, starting a chain of reactions that releases a huge amount of heat.

Radiation

Uranium is **radioactive**. This means that its nucleus is slowly decaying and giving off energy (radiation) as it does so. Some radiation occurs naturally in rocks and is responsible for the heat locked inside the Earth. The radiation from uranium is stronger, however – strong enough to damage people's health. People who are exposed to large doses of radiation can eventually develop various forms of cancer.

29

Problems of nuclear fission

In a nuclear power station, nuclear fission is used to produce heat that boils water to make steam to drive a turbine and generate electricity. Some scientists and politicians think that nuclear power stations are a good thing, but environmentalists and other scientists and politicians oppose them. What is the argument about?

The argument for nuclear power

People who support nuclear power say that renewables will never be able to supply all the electricity we need and that we should build more nuclear power stations to replace fossil fuel ones. The atomic reaction that creates the heat produces no carbon dioxide and so, they claim, nuclear power helps to reduce global warming. Only a small amount of uranium is needed to power a **nuclear reactor**, so there is enough uranium to provide a reliable and constant supply of electricity.

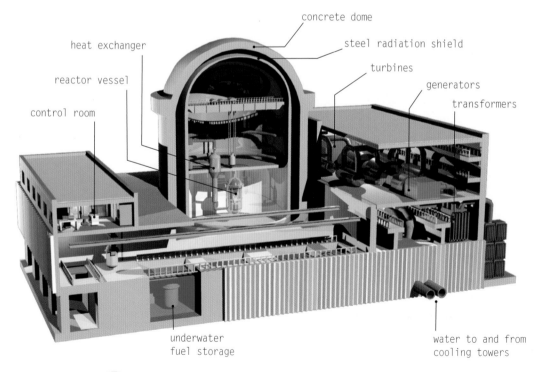

concrete dome

heat exchanger

steel radiation shield

reactor vessel

turbines

generators

control room

transformers

underwater
fuel storage

water to and from
cooling towers

The nuclear reactor is the core of a nuclear power station. So much heat is produced here that it takes large quantities of water to keep the reactor cool and stop it getting so hot that it melts.

The arguments against

The main argument against nuclear power is the radioactivity it produces. The process creates waste that remains radioactive for thousands of years, and disposing of it safely is difficult. It is often transported from the nuclear power station to other sites, risking an accident that can release radiation. There have already been many accidents inside power stations in which quantities of radiation are released into the atmosphere, endangering the health of people.

Although nuclear fission produces no carbon dioxide, nuclear power is not carbon-free. Mining uranium and making it into the rods that are used inside a reactor creates many tonnes of carbon dioxide. If the nuclear power industry expands then the demand for uranium will increase, making it more expensive. As supplies become scarcer, countries could go to war to secure their supplies, as has happened with oil.

Expense

Nuclear power is one of the most expensive ways of generating electricity. The present power stations rely on huge sums of money from the government to help pay for their building and for disposing of the waste. Opponents argue that the money would be much better spent on saving energy (see pages 40–41) and on investing in renewable sources of energy. Nuclear fission is not a renewable source of energy because no one knows for sure how much uranium is left that is worth mining.

FUTURE GENERATIONS

Nuclear waste will still be dangerously radioactive for thousands of years. Do we have the right to produce dangerous waste that future generations will have to deal with?

This person is protesting against a proposal to build a nuclear power station in South Korea.

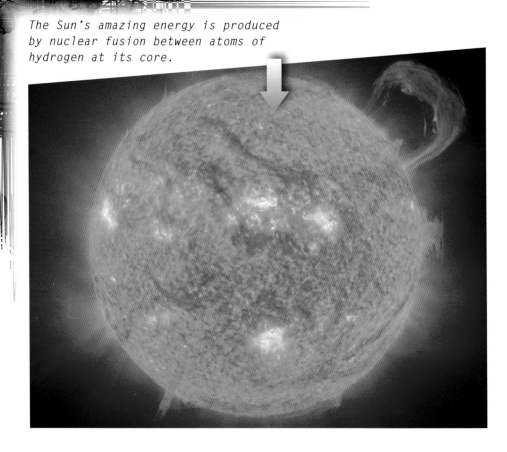

The Sun's amazing energy is produced by nuclear fusion between atoms of hydrogen at its core.

Nuclear fusion

There is a way of harnessing the energy locked up in atoms while producing much less radioactivity and not much carbon dioxide. It is called **nuclear fusion** and it reproduces the reaction that creates the Sun's energy. For decades scientists have tried to achieve the extremely high temperatures needed for this reaction – temperatures ten times hotter than the Sun!

The reaction

The reaction at the centre of nuclear fusion is actually very simple, if difficult to achieve. At very high temperatures, the nuclei of two different kinds of hydrogen atoms fuse together to produce helium and a huge amount of energy. The staggering temperature of 100 million °C (more than 180 million °F) required is not the only hurdle. The hydrogen atoms inside the reaction chamber also have to be contained and squeezed together between huge magnets. Still, the reward is immense.

One of the hydrogen atoms is made from lithium, the same metal that is used inside laptop computers. The amount of lithium in a laptop combined with the hydrogen in half a bathtub of water would produce enough energy to last the average person 30 years.

Progress

European scientists have already made a small working reaction chamber just one cubic metre (35 cubic feet) in volume. Now scientists from Europe, the United States, Russia, China, India, Japan, and South Korea are working together to build a larger reaction chamber. This generator will be ten times the size of the existing model, but it will not be big enough to produce electricity commercially. A reaction chamber big enough to produce large quantities of electricity is at least 50 years away. One of the scientists involved in the project thinks it could take nearer 100 years to achieve.

Is it worth it?

The cost of the research and development is enormous, which is why so many countries are sharing it. Nevertheless, many people argue that the money would be better spent on reducing energy waste now and on developing renewable sources of energy that we know work.

For nuclear fusion to occur, the hydrogen gas must be heated until it becomes plasma – a hot, electrically charged gas. Other gases become plasmas at much lower temperatures than hydrogen and are used, for example, in plasma televisions.

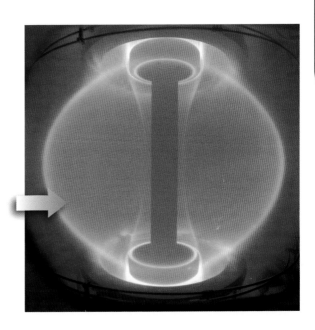

A hydrogen-fuelled future?

There is another solution to supplying the world with energy. It uses **fuel cells** and the gas hydrogen. Generating electricity from renewable sources produces no carbon dioxide but the supply of electricity is often uneven – solar power plants cannot generate electricity at night and wind turbines grind to a halt when the wind drops. Using hydrogen fuel cells along with renewable sources of energy could provide both a reliable and constant supply of electricity and the energy to fuel our transport.

A fuel cell generates electricity by combining hydrogen and oxygen from the air. The only waste gas is water vapour.

What is a fuel cell?

A fuel cell is like a battery that never needs recharging. Inside the cell, hydrogen and oxygen combine to produce water and electricity. So long as the cell is supplied with hydrogen it will go on producing electricity. At the moment the best way to produce the hydrogen is to extract it from natural gas. So the fuel cell uses natural gas to produce electricity. This is more efficient than burning natural gas to produce heat – much less energy is lost.

Another way to produce hydrogen is to use electricity to split water into hydrogen and oxygen – the reverse of the fuel cell. In this way excess energy from solar power, wind power, or wave power could be used to produce a store of hydrogen. When extra electricity is needed, a fuel cell uses some of the stored hydrogen to generate it.

An integrated system

Fuel cells running on natural gas have already been used in buildings to generate electricity and to power vehicles. Cars use the electricity generated by a fuel cell to drive an electric motor. In the future, fuel cells in buildings and in vehicles could run on hydrogen fuel instead of natural gas. Hydrogen gas could be produced using electricity generated from renewable sources. The hydrogen would then be stored as a liquid and transported to wherever it is needed. Homes could be supplied with piped hydrogen gas instead of natural gas, and at night you would use the same supply to refuel your car. But all of this is many years away.

Before such a system is possible, money has to be invested and work done to set up the pipes and the supply system. In addition the cost of fuel cells has to come down. If all of this happens, however, it could provide an unlimited supply of carbon-free energy. Fuel cells work all over the world and they could generate all the energy we could possibly need.

This bus already uses a fuel cell that extracts hydrogen from natural gas. It is the first step towards a carbon-free transport future.

The technology exists to generate electricity without producing carbon dioxide or radiation. Solar power stations, hydroelectric power stations, and wind turbines can supply most of the electricity needed. Wave power and other ideas, including some yet to be discovered perhaps, will contribute too, and hydrogen could provide a carbon-free fuel for everyone one day. We cannot, however, simply wait for technology to save us from global warming. There is not time, because global warming is happening too fast.

It takes many years to build a large power station. It can take 10-20 years from the time a nuclear power station is first proposed until it produces electricity.

Political arguments

Power stations, wind turbines, and wave machines are expensive to build and so it will take many years to switch from power stations that burn fossil fuels to carbon-free alternatives. Politicians are the people who decide what kind of power stations will be built and politicians do not agree about the best way forward. They listen to advice from many different people.

People who work for the nuclear industry want to persuade governments that nuclear power is the best way forward. Oil companies want to protect their industry and the profits they make from using oil to provide fuel for transport and power stations.

Environmentalists are not all agreed about the best options either. Some environmentalists support nuclear power but most do not. Although hydroelectric power and tidal power are carbon-free, environmentalists are concerned about their effect on local habitats and wildlife. Some local people often oppose land-based wind turbines as well as nuclear power stations.

Cost

When deciding what kind of new power station to build, governments have to take into account how much money and time it will take to build, how much electricity it will produce, and at what cost, as well as its effect on global warming. The cheapest answer is not always the best option. Land-based wind farms are cheaper to build, but large offshore turbines can supply more electricity. They also avoid local protests.

Millions of people work in the coal and oil industries, so switching from fossil fuels will endanger many people's jobs. Generating electricity from renewable sources of energy, however, will create millions of new jobs.

As governor of California, U.S.A., Arnold Schwarzenegger introduced many policies for reducing California's carbon emissions.

Time is running out

While politicians and others argue about what kind of power stations to build, time is running out. Global warming is happening faster than scientists previously predicted it would. Even if we could stop burning fossil fuels now, the extra carbon dioxide already in the atmosphere would cause the Earth's temperature to rise by about 1 °C (1.8 °F). Also, far from halting carbon dioxide output, the amount produced every year is increasing and, as the temperature of the Earth rises, it will trigger natural events that cannot be controlled, which will accelerate global warming.

Evidence of global warming

By 2006 scientists realized that global warming was happening faster than they thought. Glaciers all over the world were melting and retreating. In Greenland and Norway, for example, glaciers were several hundred metres shorter than they had been about 10 years earlier. Plants such as cereal crops were growing in Greenland, where it had previously been too cold, and birds, butterflies, and plants were also surviving in places that had previously been too cold for them.

When glaciers reach the sea, they break up and tumble into the water. Global warming is increasing the speed at which this happens.

As summers become hotter, more people use electric fans and air conditioning to stay cool.

Sea life was affected by global warming, too. As the sea becomes warmer, coral reefs become bleached – the microscopic plants on which the coral depends and which give the coral its colour cannot survive – and the coral dies. In 2006 more than half of Australia's Great Barrier Reef was affected by bleaching.

Increased demand

If we do nothing, our demand for electricity will continue to increase throughout the world and global warming itself will add to it. As the summers get hotter more homes as well as shops and offices will install air conditioning or use electric fans to keep cool. The demand for electricity will increase dramatically.

Tipping points

We cannot afford to let demand for energy increase unchecked. If we do, various **tipping points** will be reached. A tipping point is when global warming triggers a natural disaster that leads to a further increase in global warming. For example, as the Earth becomes warmer the Amazon rainforest will become drier. This means that forest fires caused by lightning will burn down vast areas of trees, leading to more global warming. When the frozen land in the **tundra** around the Arctic Ocean melts, it will release billions of tonnes of methane – one of the more destructive greenhouse gases.

Save electricity by turning off the television - don't leave it on standby.

Act now!

The quickest and easiest way to reduce greenhouses gases is to reduce the amount of energy wasted. Not only do power stations waste most of the energy in fossil fuels (see page 15), but almost a third of the energy we use is wasted. By being more economical in the way energy is used greenhouse gases can be reduced without making huge changes to our way of life. And reducing demand for electricity will make it easier to supply the electricity from renewable sources.

Saving electricity at home

- Don't leave televisions, DVD players, and computers on standby – they still use up to half the electricity they would if they were on. Switch them off.

- Don't leave phone chargers or other chargers on all night. Unplug them when they have finished charging, otherwise they go on using electricity.

- Turn off lights when leaving a room – if 40 million people turned off a light it would save the total output of two very large coal-fired power stations or five nuclear power stations.

- Use long-life light bulbs in place of **incandescent light bulbs** – long-life light bulbs use a quarter of the electricity and last eight times as long.

- Make sure machines such as dishwashers and washing machines are fully loaded and use the most economical setting.

- Always use electricity and gas as economically as possible – don't, for example, boil more water than is needed when cooking or making a cup of tea or coffee.

Carbon offsetting

Some companies have come up with the idea of 'offsetting' (cancelling out) the carbon dioxide produced by paying for something that reduces carbon dioxide emissions elsewhere. For example, using your gas and electricity bills you can calculate how many tonnes of carbon dioxide your household emitted last year. You can then pay the **carbon offsetting** company to invest in a scheme that will save the same weight of carbon dioxide. Carbon-saving schemes include planting trees, and handing out free long-life light bulbs in poor countries.

Sounds good? The problem is that the carbon dioxide emitted is already increasing global warming, whereas the carbon-saving schemes save carbon over a long period of time, and there is no guarantee that the schemes will achieve the savings they claim. It is not certain, for example, that the long-life light bulbs will be used or that the trees will survive. The biggest danger of carbon offsetting, however, is that it allows people to go on polluting because it deludes them into thinking that they can cancel out their pollution.

Long-life light bulbs are cooler than traditional light bulbs. They burn less electricity and last longer, so fewer bulbs need to be manufactured.

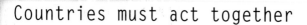

Countries must act together

Individually we can help to tackle global warming by not wasting energy, but, as the name shows, global warming is a problem that affects the whole world. It has to be tackled internationally by governments, as well as people, working together.

Who is responsible?

The map opposite shows the number of millions of tonnes of carbon dioxide emitted by the most polluting countries in the year 2000. Together they were responsible for 80 percent of the world's total emissions. The contribution of the United States, the worst polluter, is even greater per person because its population is about a quarter that of China, the next biggest polluter.

The goal

The world needs to reduce its current total emissions by half by the year 2050. To achieve this, the most polluting countries need to reduce their emissions by about 80 percent so that poorer countries can develop their economies and the carbon dioxide already in the system can be reduced. **Developing countries** will suffer the greatest effects of global warming and they need to strengthen their economies to deal with that and to make the world a fairer place.

The solution

A fair limit on emissions needs to be set for each country and agreed internationally. The Kyoto Treaty, which came into force in 2005, sets targets for the world's largest industrialized nations to cut their carbon dioxide emissions. Unfortunately the United States, responsible for 25 percent of emissions, refused to join the treaty. Since then, however, California and several other U.S. states have set up their own plans to reduce emissions.

STERN REPORT

In 2006 Sir Nicholas Stern, a British economist, showed that investing now in technology to reduce global warming will cost developed countries less than paying for the disasters that unchecked global warming will bring.

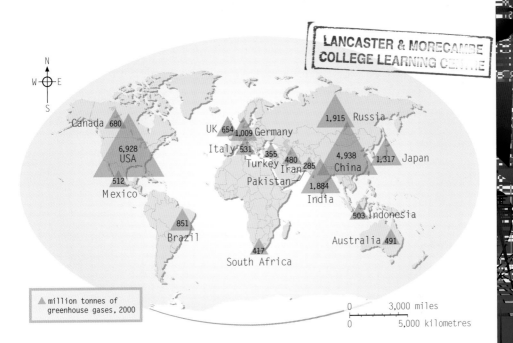

N
W ⊕ E
S

Canada 680

UK 654 1,009 Germany

1,915 Russia

6,928 USA

Italy 531   355
Turkey 480
Iran 285
Pakistan

4,938 1,317 Japan
China

512
Mexico

1,884
India

503 Indonesia

851
Brazil

Australia 491

417
South Africa

▲ million tonnes of
greenhouse gases, 2000

0   3,000 miles

0   5,000 kilometres

This shows the number of millions of tonnes of carbon dioxide emitted by the most polluting countries.

Carbon trading

When carbon dioxide emissions have been agreed, it has been suggested that carbon could be traded between countries, so that a country that emits more than its limit can buy extra carbon allowances from a country that emits less. In this way developed countries would pay money to "greener" – usually poorer – countries, which would help developing countries improve their economies. **Carbon trading** could help countries while they bring in technological changes to reduce their carbon emissions. The problem is that developed countries could simply pay for extra carbon emissions and never make the changes needed.

INCREASING EMISSIONS

Developing countries need to build more factories and power stations to improve the standard of living of their people and to get money to deal with the effects of global warming. This means that their emissions of carbon dioxide will increase. China's total emissions have already caught up with the United States, although they are still much lower when calculated per person.

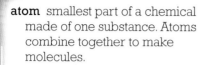

atom smallest part of a chemical made of one substance. Atoms combine together to make molecules.

carbon dioxide gas that is found mainly in the atmosphere. One molecule of carbon dioxide consists of one atom of carbon and two atoms of oxygen.

carbon offsetting balancing the carbon or carbon dioxide you have produced by paying for a reduction in carbon or carbon dioxide elsewhere

carbon trading system whereby companies and/or countries are each allocated a permitted weight of carbon (that is carbon dioxide) they can produce. Companies or countries that produce more than their allocation buy extra allowances from companies or countries that produce less than their allocation.

carbon-free without producing carbon or carbon dioxide

CHP combined heat and power. As a CHP station generates electricity, the waste heat is used to heat buildings.

CSP concentrated solar power. A CSP station uses the heat of the Sun to generate large amounts of electricity.

desalinate remove salt from seawater

developed country nation, such as the United States or Australia, with a high standard of living due to its advanced economy

developing country nation, such as Kenya or India, where most people rely on farming and are poorer than those in developed nations

electromagnet magnet produced by coiling electric wire around a metal core. When electric current flows through the wire, the metal core becomes a magnet.

electron one of the particles that make up an atom. Electrons are negatively charged and circle around the nucleus of the atom.

force push, pull or twist that is applied to an object

fossil fuels coal, oil, and natural gas. These fuels are called fossil fuels because they formed millions of years ago.

fuel something that is burned or consumed to produce energy

fuel cell device that produces electricity by combining the gas hydrogen with oxygen

gas hydrate natural gas trapped inside crystals of ice and water

global warming increase in the average temperature of the surface of the Earth

greenhouse gases gases in the atmosphere that trap the Sun's heat and so lead to global warming

grid network

hub centre of something that rotates, such as a wheel

hydroelectric power electricity generated by using the force of flowing water to turn a turbine

incandescent light bulb light bulb that makes light by heating a filament until it glows

industrialization process of mass-producing goods in factories and of providing financial and other services

isotopes variations of the same kind of atom

megawatts 1,000,000 watts or 1,000 kilowatts. A megawatt of electricity can light 10,000 100-watt light bulbs.

methane natural gas and one of the greenhouse gases.

natural gas fossil fuel produced as a gas in rocks

neutron one of the particles that make up an atom. Neutrons and protons make up the nucleus of the atom.

nitrous oxide greenhouse gas. One molecule of nitrous oxide consists of two atoms of nitrogen and one atom of oxygen.

nuclear fission splitting of an atom to produce energy

nuclear fusion joining of two atoms of hydrogen to produce helium and large amounts of energy

nuclear reactor device in which nuclear fission produces energy in a controlled chain reaction

Pelamis **wave energy converter** device that generates electricity using the movement of waves

photosynthesis process in which carbon dioxide from the air and water is combined using chlorophyll and the energy of sunlight to produce sugar. Photosynthesis mostly takes place in the leaves of green plants and produces oxygen as a waste gas.

photovoltaic cell device that generates electricity using sunlight

power station building or complex of devices that generates large amounts of electricity

proton one of the particles that make up an atom. Protons and neutrons make up the nucleus of the atom.

radioactive emitting energy as the nucleus of certain atoms, such as uranium, decay

refinery building where oil is refined, or separated, into different substances

renewable able to be renewed and so everlasting. Some forms of energy are said to be renewable because they will not run out.

resources materials that can be used to create wealth

silt dust or powder that settles to the bottom of a liquid

synthetic materials materials, such as plastic, nylon, and acrylic, that are made from oil

tidal power station power station that generates electricity using the movement of the tides

tidal stream farm group of turbines that generate electricity using the movement of the tide or currents

tipping point critical point in a changing situation that triggers further unavoidable changes

tundra treeless area of land that borders the Arctic and is also found just below the permanent snows of high mountains

turbine device that rotates to generate electricity

uranium substance that is radioactive and which is used in nuclear fission to generate electricity

water cycle continuous circulation of water between the atmosphere, the land, and the oceans

water vapour water in the form of a gas

wind turbine device that uses the force of the wind to generate electricity

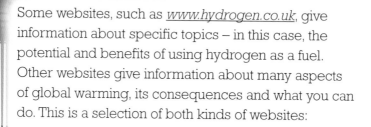

Further information

Some websites, such as _www.hydrogen.co.uk_, give information about specific topics – in this case, the potential and benefits of using hydrogen as a fuel. Other websites give information about many aspects of global warming, its consequences and what you can do. This is a selection of both kinds of websites:

Global warming

www.bbc.co.uk/climate/
Website produced by the BBC. It explains simply and clearly the greenhouse effect, the impact of global warming, and the adaptations we shall need to make.

www.epa.gov/climatechange/
Website of the U.S. Environmental Protection Agency, which explains global warming and its effect on the environment and eco systems and suggests various things you can do.

www.ecocentre.org.uk/global-warming.html
Explains the greenhouse effect and where greenhouse gases come from.

climate.wri.org/topic_data_trends.cfm
Gives a world map in which the area of each country is in proportion to the weight of carbon dioxide it emits.

www.energyquest.ca.gov/story/chapter08.html
Explains how coal, oil, and natural gas were formed.

www.commondreams.org/headlines06/0312-03.htm
Gives an article published in the _Observer_ newspaper about tipping points in the Arctic and how they will accelerate global warming.

www.climatehotmap.org/
A website that gives a map showing early warning signs of global warming in different continents. Produced by several organizations including World Resources Institute, Environmental Defense, and World Wildlife Fund.

www.earthinstitute.columbia.edu/crosscutting/climate.html
Website of the Earth Institute at Columbia University, U.S..A. It outlines the consequences of global warming and suggests some things you can do.

www.greenpeace.org.uk/climate/climatechange/index.cfm
Website of UK environmental campaigning organization, Greenpeace, with facts and predictions concerning global warming.

www.sierraclub.org/globalwarming/qa/
Website covering global warming and things you can do about it.

www.climatecrisis.net/
Website for the film _An Inconvenient Truth_, which includes facts about global warming and things you can do.

Wind power

www.riverdeep.net/current/2002/04/040802t_power.jhtml
Website for teachers about wave and wind power in the United States.

www.awea.org/faq/wwt_basics.html
Website of the American Wind Energy Association, which tells you how wind turbines work and how much electricity they provide.

www.capewind.org/
Website of Cape Wind, the company building America's first offshore wind farm off the coast of Cape Cod, Massachusetts, U.S.A.

MAKING THE CLOUDS THICKER

Dr Salter (see page 25) and U.S. scientist John Latham have invented a novel way of combatting global warming. Stratocumulus clouds are thick, bubbly, low-lying clouds, which reflect sunlight back into space. Spraying salt water into them makes them thicker and more reflective. The scientists propose using 50 yachts powered only by wind. Each yacht would need to spray 500 kilogrammes (1,100 pounds) of seawater into the clouds every minute.

www.edp24.co.uk/Windfarms/asp/where/Yarmouth_C2iic.asp
Website giving information about Scroby Sands wind farm off the coast of Norfolk in the UK.

Water power

www.fujitaresearch.com/reports/tidalpower.html
Website giving information on technology for generating electricity from waves and tides.

www.wavegen.com/index.html
Website of Wavegen, the Scottish-based company that is responsible for the wave power generator on the Isle of Islay. The site includes a web cam that shows you the waves around the generator.

www.wavegen.com/about_wave_energy_info_schools_wave_whistles.htm
This section of Wavegen's website is for schools and includes instructions for making a model that shows how wave power works.

www.worldenergy.org/wec-geis/publications/reports/ser/hydro/hydro.asp
Website of the World Energy Council, giving information of use and potential of water power around the world.

Solar power

www.solarpaces.org/CSP_Technology/csp_technology.htm
Explains how solar power can be used to generate large amounts of electricity.

www.nrdc.org/air/energy/renewables/solar.asp
Website produced by the US Natural Resources Defense Council which gives information about all kinds of solar power.

www.worldenergy.org/wec-geis/publications/reports/ser/solar/solar.asp
Website of the World Energy Council, giving information about the possibilities of using solar power around the world.

Nuclear power

www.foe.co.uk/campaigns/climate/issues/climate_change/index.html
Website of the UK campaigning organizations Friends of the Earth, which gives information about climate change and the problems of nuclear energy.

www.jet.efda.org
Website of the Joint European Torus, which is developing nuclear fusion for Europe. Click on "fusion basics" for an explanation of how it all works.

Hydrogen fuel

www.hydrogen.co.uk/h2/hydrogen.htm
Gives diagram showing how hydrogen could be produced from renewable sources of electricity and used to power buildings and transport.

Carbon offsetting

www.carbonfootprint.com/calculator.html
Website that allows you to calculate how much carbon your family produces.

*I*ndex